Prayers

and

Promises

for

Christmas

GW00418414

Prayers

and

Promises

for
Christmas

*Biblical Encouragement
for the Holiday Season*

Jennifer Hahn

BARBOUR
PUBLISHING

Print ISBN 978-1-61626-855-8

eBook Editions:
Adobe Digital Edition (.epub) 978-1-62029-100-9
Kindle and MobiPocket Edition (.prc) 978-1-62029-101-6

All scripture quotations are taken from the King James Version of the Bible.

Published by Barbour Publishing, Inc., P.O. Box 719, Uhrichsville, Ohio 44683 www.barbourbooks.com

Our mission is to publish and distribute inspirational products offering exceptional value and biblical encouragement to the masses.

Member of the
Evangelical Christian
Publishers Association

Printed in the United States of America.

CONTENTS

INTRODUCTION

God's promises have richly blessed Christians through the ages. They have offered solutions to problems, strength during trials, and inspiration for the Christian life.

In the pages that follow, we provide prayers—specifically for the Christmas season—based on many of scripture's promises. Whether you are struggling with busyness or contentment, wish to celebrate the traditions or goodwill of the season, or need to draw close to God the Father's loving heart, take hold of the truths in scripture and offer a heartfelt prayer.

These "starter prayers" may be helpful for family devotions or small-group Bible studies. But most of all we hope they will draw you closer to God and inspire your own prayers. As you pray, feel free to add your personal needs, those of your family and friends, or the concerns of your small group or congregation.

Pray, and experience the truth of God's promise to Jeremiah: "Call unto me, and I will answer thee, and show thee great and mighty things, which thou knowest not" (Jeremiah 33:3).

ADVENT

The Promise of Immanuel

Therefore the Lord himself shall give you a sign;
Behold, a virgin shall conceive, and bear a son,
and shall call his name Immanuel.
ISAIAH 7:14

Father God, You made a promise through the prophet Isaiah—a promise You fulfilled seven hundred years later with the birth of Your Son, Jesus Christ.

Only You could make a virgin conceive a child. Only You could offer salvation through that child. Only You would step into Your creation as a human being—*Immanuel* means "God with us"—and experience the life we live on this earth.

I thank You, Father, for the promise of a child—the virgin's Son who would later die on the cross for my sins.

Promise Fulfilled

And, behold, thou shalt conceive in thy womb,
and bring forth a son, and shalt call his name JESUS.
LUKE 1:31

Father, You had promised in Isaiah's time that You would send a son, a child to be born to a virgin. And centuries later, to a young Jewish virgin named Mary, You sent an angel with this promise: "Behold, thou shalt conceive in thy womb, and bring forth a son, and shalt call his name JESUS."

Lord, Your word is true, no matter how many years may pass. Your promises can always be relied on. Your predictions always come true.

Thank You, Father, for the baby boy You conceived in Mary's womb—the Son named Jesus who would save His people from their sins.

Who Jesus Is

For unto us a child is born, unto us a son is given:
and the government shall be upon his shoulder:
and his name shall be called Wonderful, Counsellor,
The mighty God, The everlasting Father,
The Prince of Peace.
ISAIAH 9:6

Lord, I love the names of Jesus in this verse:

"Wonderful" makes me think of all the things I enjoy most.

"Counsellor" tells me that the Christmas child is wise, compassionate, and full of good advice.

Knowing that Jesus is "The mighty God" gives me confidence to face any challenge—and knowing that He is "The everlasting Father" reminds me of His love and concern for me as His child.

And when I see the title "Prince of Peace," I think of the difference Jesus can make in the world—in individual hearts and among nations—if we only allow Him to work in our lives. Thank You, Father, for this Son You've given!

Where Jesus Comes From

And there shall come forth a rod out of the stem of Jesse,
and a Branch shall grow out of his roots.
ISAIAH 11:1

Father God, this "Wonderful, Counsellor. . .mighty God. . .everlasting Father. . .Prince of Peace" You sent to earth has been with You for all eternity. But He became human through a very specific family, the line of Israel's King David.

You had promised David—the youngest son of a man named Jesse—that his kingdom would be an everlasting one. With Jesus' birth, You brought forth a rod from the stem of Jesse, a branch out of Jesse's roots. And You began the fulfillment of yet another promise.

You tell us where Jesus came from to encourage us with where *we're* going.

Jesus Is Real

Hereby know ye the Spirit of God: Every spirit that confesseth that Jesus Christ is come in the flesh is of God.
1 JOHN 4:2

Lord, You're always thinking of my needs: You give me confidence in my faith when I believe in the birth of Jesus Christ.

There are always doubters, Father, and some of them say that Jesus wasn't truly human—that He was just a spirit, some kind of illusion. And if He wasn't truly human, He couldn't possibly affect our human condition.

But Jesus *did* come in the flesh—born outside a real Bethlehem inn, raised in the real town of Nazareth, ministering as an adult from the real village of Capernaum. . .and dying on a very real cross outside Jerusalem.

May I never forget, Father, that Jesus is *real*.

To Defeat Death

*Forasmuch then as the children are partakers of flesh and
blood, he also himself likewise took part of the same;
that through death he might destroy him
that had the power of death, that is, the devil.*
HEBREWS 2:14

Father, why would You send Your own Son to live
among sinful people, ultimately dying a cruel death
on the cross?

This verse answers our questions: You allowed
Jesus to die to break the power of the devil. Satan
thought he'd defeated You, but Jesus' Resurrection
proved that He was not in any way bound by death.
And with the eternal life Jesus offers, neither are we!

Thank You, Lord, for sending Jesus to earth. Born
in humble circumstances in the tiny, insignificant
village of Bethlehem, Jesus lived a perfect life, died
a sacrificial death, and purchased my salvation with
His blood. I need never fear death. Jesus has defeated it!

BLESSINGS

Listening to Your Voice

*And it shall come to pass, if thou shalt hearken diligently
unto the voice of the LORD thy God, to observe
and to do all his commandments which I command
thee this day, that the LORD thy God will set thee
on high above all nations of the earth:
And all these blessings shall come on thee, and overtake thee,
if thou shalt hearken unto the voice of the LORD thy God.*
DEUTERONOMY 28:1–2

Lord, it is clear that we need to listen to Your voice. Sometimes the noise of life drowns out Your voice, and then we must confess that we haven't been listening closely to You. You will not speak louder to compete for our attention—You patiently wait for us to quiet ourselves and listen.

I want to be a diligent listener. As Mary, Joseph, and the shepherds heard Your voice, may I be ready to hear the message You have for me. I thank You for the blessing You have promised to those who listen to and obey Your voice.

Blessed Forgiveness

Blessed is he whose transgression is forgiven,
whose sin is covered. Blessed is the man unto whom the LORD
imputeth not iniquity, and in whose spirit there is no guile.
PSALM 32:1–2

Father God, I am so thankful that You came to earth to die for my sins. You arrived as a baby, then spent Your life preparing to take the sins of the world onto Yourself on the cross. Your blood has covered my sins.

What freedom I enjoy in Your forgiveness! Yet what a sacrifice You made to bring about that freedom. You suffered physical pain, You were mocked, and Your friends betrayed You. But You did it all as a gift for me, because of Your love. Thank You, Lord, for the blessing of forgiveness.

Spiritual Blessings

Blessed be the God and Father of our Lord Jesus Christ,
who hath blessed us with all spiritual blessings
in heavenly places in Christ.
EPHESIANS 1:3

Lord God, we bless You for all Your great works. You have done so much for us, and it is our honor to bless You.

You sent Your Son to live among people then ultimately die for the sin of all humanity. You removed the penalty of eternal death by offering eternal life.

You have made us new creatures. Our old way of living is gone, and we now walk in Your way. You protect us from the evil that surrounds us.

You love us with Your everlasting love.

We bless Your name!

Showers of Blessing

And I will make them and the places round about my hill a blessing; and I will cause the shower to come down in his season; there shall be showers of blessing.
EZEKIEL 34:26

Lord, Your "showers of blessing" come in many ways. They can be a literal rain after a period of drought. They can be new employment opportunities following times of unemployment. They can be increased wealth after financial hardships.

We trust that You know what is best for every situation. We often think *we* know the answer to our difficulties—but may we believe that the blessing You bestow is exactly what we need. And may we always remember to thank You for those blessings.

Simeon's Blessing

And Simeon blessed them, and said unto Mary his mother,
Behold, this child is set for the fall and rising again of many
in Israel; and for a sign which shall be spoken against.
LUKE 2:34

Father God, what joy Simeon must have felt in being the one chosen to bless Jesus, Mary, and Joseph. He had long awaited the birth of the Messiah—and trusted he would one day lay his hands on the Promised One to pray a blessing over Him. Your Spirit had spoken to Simeon, and he'd been assured he would not die before seeing the Messiah.

Simeon's faith and patience is a wonderful example to us, Lord. May we wait patiently, in faith, for the work You have for us to do.

Blessed in Persecution

Blessed are ye, when men shall revile you, and persecute you, and shall say all manner of evil against you falsely, for my sake. Rejoice, and be exceeding glad: for great is your reward in heaven: for so persecuted they the prophets which were before you.
MATTHEW 5:11–12

Lord, I ask for courage when others mock me because of my love for You. Your Word says that the prophets who foretold Your life and work were persecuted, too. They must have become weary at times, from the laughter and jeering. But each message would be proven true—You *did* come as a baby, born in Bethlehem, fulfilling prophecy after prophecy.

Please help me to find joy and gladness in spite of the persecution. I am not ashamed of You, Jesus—You humbled Yourself to come to earth for me. I will boldly live for You.

BUSYNESS

Resting in the Lord

Rest in the LORD, and wait patiently for him: fret not thyself because of him who prospereth in his way, because of the man who bringeth wicked devices to pass.
PSALM 37:7

Heavenly Father, at times it takes *effort* to rest in You. Especially at this time of year, I look at others around me who seem to get whatever they want—and I have to admit that it sometimes bothers me. And then there are those who seem to succeed even when living contrary to Your ways.

Lord, please quiet my mind when I compare what seems to be the success or wealth of others with my lack of it. I want to choose to rest in You, to wait patiently, and not to fret. Only then will I have true success.

God's Presence

And he said, My presence shall go with thee,
and I will give thee rest.
EXODUS 33:14

Lord God, during this season, we celebrate the gift of Your presence here on earth, when You arrived as a baby. But You did not remove Your presence when You returned to heaven—You promised that the Holy Spirit would come to be with us. You have not left us alone!

What a comfort in this promise. In this declaration, You have promised the rest we so desperately desire. We don't need to chase after You or compete for Your attention. You are with us continually! I can find true rest in that promise.

Your Yoke, My Rest

Come unto me, all ye that labour and are heavy laden,
and I will give you rest. Take my yoke upon you,
and learn of me; for I am meek and lowly in heart:
and ye shall find rest unto your souls.
MATTHEW 11:28–29

Lord, I certainly have moments when I feel labored and heavy laden—especially with all the tasks I need to complete today. In these times, it seems as if I am too weak to do much of anything, and You tell me to take up Your yoke?

But only in taking that step will I find true rest.

Teach me more about Yourself, Lord. I have so much to learn, but I am eager to draw closer to You.

Thank You for desiring me—to want to be yoked with me. The rest for my soul will be so sweet.

A Desert Place

And he said unto them, Come ye yourselves apart into a desert place, and rest a while: for there were many coming and going, and they had no leisure so much as to eat.
MARK 6:31

Lord Jesus, You recognized the need for rest as You traveled with Your disciples. There were many demands on Your time as You walked this earth.

My pace is much too fast at times, and my priorities get out of order. I need to find my own "desert place" when I can rest—a place free of all the demands on my time. Please help me to find that place, to commit to resting, to free myself from the distractions that normally consume my time. And may I set my priorities so that my life will honor You.

The Day of Rest

*Six days thou shalt work, but on the seventh day thou shalt
rest: in earing time and in harvest thou shalt rest.*
EXODUS 34:21

Lord, at the beginning of time, You mandated a day to rest. I ask for Your forgiveness for those times I've treated Your day of rest like the six that preceded it. My schedule is so full (often too full!), and I tell myself I can use *Your* day to catch up on obligations I've failed to meet.

Please help me to plan my schedule wisely for the six days of work. Then may I set aside the seventh day to rest, as You have commanded.

Be Still

Be still, and know that I am God: I will be exalted
among the heathen, I will be exalted in the earth.
PSALM 46:10

Father, with the pace of life, I wonder if I can really be *still*. There is so much I need to get done, but only twenty-four hours each day in which to complete my to-do list.

But You haven't asked me to *think* about being still, or to *hope* to be still. You've simply commanded that I be still. Even if I need to schedule a time to be still, I will devote myself to doing so.

I thank You that You are God and Lord over all—even over my schedule.

CHILDREN

A Heritage and Reward

Lo, children are an heritage of the LORD:
and the fruit of the womb is his reward.
PSALM 127:3

Father, we would expect that Jesus, as a child, would be labeled a "heritage" and a "reward." But in this psalm, You've declared that *children*—all children—are a heritage and reward.

What an immense joy to be referred to as Your reward! Some days I don't feel like I could be anyone's reward—especially *Yours*. Yet You never lie, so I can place full trust in the fact that You consider *me* Your reward. Thank You for placing such a high value on me!

Faith of a Child

Suffer the little children to come unto me, and forbid them not: for of such is the kingdom of God. Verily I say unto you, Whosoever shall not receive the kingdom of God as a little child, he shall not enter therein. And he took them up in his arms, put his hands upon them, and blessed them.
MARK 10:14–16

Lord God, while Jesus walked the earth, it was apparent He had a deep level of love and compassion for children. He welcomed them, held them, and blessed them. He demanded they be permitted to come close to Him.

Children have a basic faith that is so refreshing, and even more evident at Christmastime. Jesus spoke of receiving the kingdom of God "as a little child." Please deepen my faith, Lord, so I can trust completely in You. May I receive the kingdom of God with childlike faith.

God's Children

The Spirit itself beareth witness with our spirit, that we are the children of God: And if children, then heirs; heirs of God, and joint-heirs with Christ; if so be that we suffer with him, that we may be also glorified together.
ROMANS 8:16–17

Lord, Your Word says Your Spirit bears witness with our spirit, identifying us as Your children. But then it goes beyond that. As Your children, we are also considered heirs of God—and not only heirs, but "joint-heirs with Christ." We share in the glory with Jesus Himself!

In sharing in His glory, though, we also share in the suffering—not alone but *with Christ*. Thank You, Lord, for naming me an heir, for sharing Your inheritance with me. Your ways are wonderful.

Receiving God

And he took a child, and set him in the midst of them: and
when he had taken him in his arms, he said unto them,
Whosoever shall receive one of such children in my name,
receiveth me: and whosoever shall receive me,
receiveth not me, but him that sent me.
MARK 9:36–37

Lord, again You showed the magnitude of the love You have for children. In the middle of a crowd, You singled out one child and used him as an object lesson, so that those around You—and we, generations later—could better understand Your words.

Jesus, You lovingly took a child in Your arms and stated that whoever would receive such a child would, in the same way, receive You. Yet in receiving You, we would ultimately receive the one who sent You, God the Father.

I believe, Lord, and receive You.

A Predetermined Plan

Before I formed thee in the belly I knew thee; and
before thou camest forth out of the womb I sanctified thee,
and I ordained thee a prophet unto the nations.
JEREMIAH 1:5

Lord Jesus, one thing humans all have in common—and with You, as well—is that we began life on this earth as children. At birth, we are fully dependent on others for our basic needs. And we are nurtured through our formative years until our age of independence.

Yet You knew us far before our births. You had a plan for Your children before they were even formed "in the belly." What a comfort to know that my birth was no surprise to You— that You had a plan for me before I was even conceived. Please keep me in step with Your plan for my life.

Forgiven Children

I write unto you, little children, because your sins
are forgiven you for his name's sake.
1 JOHN 2:12

Father God, I thank You for considering us
Your children. We recognize that we are indeed
Your children—our full reliance is on You, our
Father. We feed on Your Word. You protect us.
You discipline us when we lose our way. You are
always ready to help us when we call.

I thank You that You forgive me unconditionally when I sin against You. Help me
to extend that same forgiveness to others who
offend me. May Your name be glorified in the
unity of Your children. We long for the day
when we're with You.

CONTENTMENT

Content in Christ

Not that I speak in respect of want: for I have learned, in whatsoever state I am, therewith to be content. I know both how to be abased, and I know how to abound: every where and in all things I am instructed both to be full and to be hungry, both to abound and to suffer need.
PHILIPPIANS 4:11–12

Father, some people seem to have everything they need, while others don't have enough. There are seasons of life when everything goes well, and others when there is destitution.

The apostle Paul wrote that he experienced both extremes. He had times of plenty, and he had times of need. Yet in either situation, he was able to be content.

May I rest in You this season, knowing that whatever my circumstances—rich or poor, hungry or full—I can learn to be content.

A Desire for Godliness

But godliness with contentment is great gain.
For we brought nothing into this world,
and it is certain we can carry nothing out.
And having food and raiment let us be therewith content.
1 TIMOTHY 6:6–8

Lord, during this time of year, many will exchange gifts with friends and family. But as special as those gifts might be, when our life here on earth is over, not one of us will take them with us.

We thank You for the food and clothing You provide for us—the daily blessing for our daily needs. Help us to be thankful for what we have, and not to worry about accumulating more. We ask for godliness, so that we can be truly content.

Covet-free Conversation

*Let your conversation be without covetousness; and be
content with such things as ye have: for he hath said,
I will never leave thee, nor forsake thee.*
HEBREWS 13:5

Father, this is the time of year when people
make their "wish lists." Discussions turn to what
will be "under the tree" on Christmas morning.
Covetousness can run rampant.

Please, Lord, I pray that You will guard my
tongue in my conversations. May I only speak
positive, kind, contented words. Guard my
heart, too, that I do not give covetousness a
place there.

I thank You that You are always with me and
will never leave me. May my actions prove that
I believe Your Holy Spirit dwells within me.

Perfect Peace

*Thou wilt keep him in perfect peace, whose mind is
stayed on thee: because he trusteth in thee.*
ISAIAH 26:3

Lord, Your peace will reign in the one who keeps
his mind fixed on You. That promise can settle
anxious thoughts and times of doubt.

When Mary was told she would give birth to
Jesus, anxiety and doubt could have overtaken
her. But even though it was difficult for her
to understand, she expressed only faith. Mary
believed her experience would be just as the
heavenly messenger had described.

Lord, help me to keep my mind on You,
so that I—like Mary—may experience Your
perfect peace.

Strengthened in Weakness

*Therefore I take pleasure in infirmities, in reproaches,
in necessities, in persecutions, in distresses for Christ's sake:
for when I am weak, then am I strong.*
2 CORINTHIANS 12:10

Father, it's difficult to "take pleasure" in times of infirmity, reproach, need, persecution, and distress. Those times usually are stressful and upsetting—so to find pleasure in them seems impossible. Yet You have promised to carry us through even the most difficult of circumstances. And it is in these times that we are humbled. We are strengthened because of the weaknesses that draw us to You.

May I be a light for You, Lord, even in the midst of difficulty.

Treasure in Heaven

Lay not up for yourselves treasures upon earth,
where moth and rust doth corrupt, and where thieves break
through and steal: But lay up for yourselves treasures in
heaven, where neither moth nor rust doth corrupt,
and where thieves do not break through nor steal:
For where your treasure is, there will your heart be also.
MATTHEW 6:19–21

Lord, You told us not to lay up treasures for ourselves on earth, but rather in heaven. You don't oppose possessions on earth, but You want us to keep them in perspective.

The wise men brought You gifts of gold, frankincense, and myrrh. Those treasures were meant as a gift for the one they journeyed a great distance to see. Yet the true treasure was the first gift they gave—their worship, when they fell before You.

Help me to keep the right perspective, focusing on the treasures that will last forever.

FAMILY

Training Up Children

For I know him, that he will command his children and his household after him, and they shall keep the way of the LORD, to do justice and judgment; that the LORD may bring upon Abraham that which he hath spoken of him.
GENESIS 18:19

Father God, Your plan is for each parent who knows You to train their children in Your ways. Throughout history You've called parents to bring up their children in the knowledge of You—reading the Word together, providing instruction, and communicating with You in prayer.

Lord, in this season, the world emphasizes children—and may I teach them both by my actions and my words. May the children learn to live what they learn, so that they, in turn, can teach their children.

Submitting to Others

See then that ye walk circumspectly, not as fools, but as wise…
submitting yourselves one to another in the fear of God.
EPHESIANS 5:15, 21

Lord God, we are to submit to others—but that is so difficult, especially with family members. Why is it so hard to say "I was wrong" or "I'm sorry"?

Please help me overcome my pride. When I am wrong, Lord, help me admit it. I don't want to ruin family relationships because of my arrogance. Teach me to submit to others with a heart of love, so we can remain unified. Make my family ties stronger.

We Will Serve the Lord

And if it seem evil unto you to serve the LORD, choose you this day whom ye will serve; whether the gods which your fathers served that were on the other side of the flood, or the gods of the Amorites, in whose land ye dwell: but as for me and my house, we will serve the LORD.

JOSHUA 24:15

Father, I know from reading the Old Testament that many people strayed into the worship of false gods. They were pursuing something they thought was right, but they were sadly misguided—and that brought trouble and pain.

Lord, I choose You to be head of my household. May I and my whole family grow closer to You each day. Keep us on Your path, Father. We ask for Your leading in our lives and in our home.

Living Together in Unity

Behold, how good and how pleasant it is for brethren to dwell together in unity!

PSALM 133:1

Lord God, family sometimes feels like the last place unity can dwell. We have different personalities, different issues, and different schedules. Christmas plays, concerts, and parties all demand our attention this time of year.

Father, please bring unity to my family. May we speak kindly to each other and strive to love. May we schedule our activities so we can enjoy quality time together. I ask that my household will be one that is pleasant and unified.

A Holy and Pleasing Way

I will behave myself wisely in a perfect way.
O when wilt thou come unto me?
I will walk within my house with a perfect heart.
PSALM 101:2

Father, that word "perfect" can distort my interpretation of this verse. I know that only You are perfect—and Jesus, who came to earth as God in man, is the only human who has led a perfect life.

But "perfect" here means "without blame"— and I ask that You will strengthen my family to live a life that is holy and pleasing to You. We will fail, but You will forgive. May we strive to live "perfect" lives, knowing that You will reward us in heaven for our efforts within our homes.

May this family be blessed as we each live holy lives, drawing closer to You.

The Leader Cornelius

There was a certain man in Caesarea called Cornelius,
a centurion of the band called the Italian band,
a devout man, and one that feared God with all his house,
which gave much alms to the people,
and prayed to God alway.
ACTS 10:1–2

Lord, Your Word is full of examples for us to follow. We read of Cornelius, a leader who trusted in You. He instructed his household in Your ways; he was called devout; he gave to those in need; he was in constant communication with You.

This man inspires me to live a more godly life. I want to trust in You; have a reputation for following You; give to others; live a life of prayer. May my family see my example—and, as a result, want to grow in their relationship with You, too.

GENEROSITY

Feasting Together

But when thou makest a feast, call the poor, the maimed, the lame, the blind: and thou shalt be blessed; for they cannot recompense thee: for thou shalt be recompensed at the resurrection of the just.
LUKE 14:13–14

Heavenly Father, this is the time of year when families and friends gather for meals together. There is usually an abundance of food, and the time sharing fellowship is so special. We have so many happy memories of those times spent around a table.

Help me to remember those who may *not* have friends or family with whom they can share a meal. May I focus on those poor or disadvantaged this year. Lead me to someone I can invite to a special meal.

The Power of Giving

Withhold not good from them to whom it is due,
when it is in the power of thine hand to do it.
Say not unto thy neighbour, Go, and come again,
and to morrow I will give; when thou hast it by thee.
PROVERBS 3:27–28

Lord, I have tried to prepare my household for this holiday season. I have purchased the "extras" I need on hand.

You tell me to not withhold good when it's in my power to give. You say not to tell neighbors to come back later if they need to borrow something now. Sometimes I want to hold on to those things, just in case *I* may need them. But if I put myself in their place, I would appreciate the assistance.

May I not dwell on the "giving up" but rather on the "helping out"—and do as You have commanded.

Two Minus One

He answereth and saith unto them,
He that hath two coats,
let him impart to him that hath none;
and he that hath meat, let him do likewise.
LUKE 3:11

Father, You have blessed me greatly. But there are others who lack even the basic necessities—clothing or food. Some of them need fare for bus transportation or assistance of other kinds.

I ask, Lord, that I will have a heart of generosity—that I can be willing to donate the clothing I don't need or the extra food that can nourish a hungry person. And please help me to give of my time to meet the needs of others.

A Giving Blessing

Give, and it shall be given unto you; good measure, pressed down, and shaken together, and running over, shall men give into your bosom. For with the same measure that ye mete withal it shall be measured to you again.
LUKE 6:38

Lord, as Your follower, I know I should always be ready to help others in need. There have been times in my life that *I've* needed assistance—and there are times that I am able to help others.

You have promised, Father, that You will give to those who are generous with others. I don't want to give for that reason—but I do thank You for Your blessing when I obey Your command.

Father, I ask that you make generosity a natural part of me.

Honor the Poor

He that oppresseth the poor reproacheth his Maker:
but he that honoureth him hath mercy on the poor.
PROVERBS 14:31

Lord God, may I never be guilty of oppressing the poor. I would never intend to dishonor them, nor to reproach You.

Help me, instead, to have mercy on those in need, to put them in a place of honor. Direct me to someone I can encourage for Your glory, Lord.

Today, may I be generous with my finances—and my honor.

Answering the Call

*Give to him that asketh thee, and from him that
would borrow of thee turn not thou away.*
MATTHEW 5:42

Father, at this time of year, so many people and
organizations are asking for donations. The needs
are countless. And since I am not able to give to
each one, I ask that You will give me wisdom to
know with whom I should share my possessions.
You know who would benefit most from my
generosity.

I want to be used of You, Lord. I ask that You
will give me the opportunity to bless someone
who requests assistance.

GIFTS

Cheerful Giving

*Every man according as he purposeth in his heart,
so let him give; not grudgingly, or of necessity:
for God loveth a cheerful giver.*
2 CORINTHIANS 9:7

Heavenly Father, You have asked that Your children give gifts from a heart of joy, not out of duty or reluctance. Sometimes I give with a spirit of gladness—but at times, giving can become routine or mundane. You've cautioned me against that. Your desire is that I give *cheerfully*.

Thank You, Lord, for Your blessings, that I can give something back for Your use. Please help me to give with a heart overflowing with sincere joy.

Able and Willing

Every man shall give as he is able, according to the blessing of the LORD thy God which he hath given thee.
DEUTERONOMY 16:17

Lord, please help me to remember to give as I am able—to give according to the blessings You have showered on me. It's so easy to get carried away in buying things then find that I don't have much left for giving. But everything that You have entrusted to me is Yours.

I want to give according to my ability, to help You meet the needs of others.

Gifts of the Wise Men

*And when they were come into the house,
they saw the young child with Mary his mother,
and fell down, and worshipped him: and when they had
opened their treasures, they presented unto him gifts;
gold, and frankincense and myrrh.*

MATTHEW 2:11

Father God, as the wise men left their homes—setting out on a journey to an unknown place—they must have had great anticipation. They were searching for the King of the Jews, quoting the prophecy that said that He would be born in Bethlehem.

The wise men joyfully followed the star to where Jesus was—and immediately bowed and worshipped Him. Then they presented their gifts of gold, frankincense, and myrrh.

Lord, may I—like the wise men—be eager to give what I have to others.

The Gift of God

For by grace are ye saved through faith;
and that not of yourselves: it is the gift of God: not of works,
lest any man should boast.
EPHESIANS 2:8–9

Lord, we praise You for the gift of Your Son. He died for all people, without discrimination, to give us a life free of condemnation. Because of Your love, we are now forgiven—and can look forward to eternal life with You.

We did nothing to bring about Your love, nor could we ever do anything to deserve it. All the glory belongs to You alone. We praise You and thank You for the gift You freely and willingly gave.

Gifts in the Body

For as we have many members in one body,
and all members have not the same office: so we,
being many, are one body in Christ,
and every one members one of another.
ROMANS 12:4–5

Father, these verses say that we're all different, yet necessary to the body of Christ.

I think of what happens in a children's Nativity play at church: Most of the kids want the role of Mary or Joseph. Yet if nobody played the part of a shepherd or wise man, the story would be lacking.

The spiritual gifts You've entrusted to us are for *Your* glory—so that we as one body can work together to accomplish Your work. Lord, I am grateful for the gifts You have given me. I choose to be an effective member of Your body.

Good and Perfect Gifts

Every good gift and every perfect gift is from above,
and cometh down from the Father of lights,
with whom is no variableness, neither shadow of turning.
JAMES 1:17

Father, You cannot change. You are steadfast. You will not throw us into confusion by adjusting Your ways.

Thank You for giving us good and perfect gifts. Help me to remember that these gifts are good and perfect in Your eyes. I sometimes choose ways that I think are good and perfect— but You determine what is best. May I put my complete trust in You.

Lord, we treasure the gifts we receive from You.

GOD THE FATHER

Our Adoptive Father

For ye have not received the spirit of bondage again to fear,
but ye have received the Spirit of adoption,
whereby we cry, Abba, Father.
ROMANS 8:15

Lord, You have adopted me—You chose me! I was a sinner, yet You loved me enough to send Your Son to die as a sacrifice for me. I can't comprehend how painful that must have been for You. You were separated from Your Son, even turning away as He took on the pain and sin of all mankind.

But you endured all that so I could call You *Abba*—"Daddy." You replace my fear with a heart full of love for You, Father!

Glorifying the Father

Let your light so shine before men,
that they may see your good works,
and glorify your Father which is in heaven.
MATTHEW 5:16

Father God, You have said that I am to be a shining light. Because You *are* the Light and I am in You, I can share Your light with those around me.

The works I do are not good in themselves; they are only good if they originate in You. Help me to do Your good works, so that You can receive the glory due You.

I want to point others to You, Lord. May my light shine brightly and my works show evidence of You.

The Father and Son Are One

Believest thou not that I am in the Father,
and the Father in me? the words that I speak unto you
I speak not of myself: but the Father that dwelleth in me,
he doeth the works.

JOHN 14:10

Lord God, Your Son claimed to be one with You. I know that's no idle claim—it is truth. He is in You, and You are in Him. You sent Him to earth to do Your will, and He was perfectly willing to do that.

What a homecoming it must have been, Father, when Your Son returned to You. He had been separated from You, bearing the ugly mark of sin—but when His work was done, He returned to Your side in heaven.

Thank You for giving us Your Son.

The Pleasure of the Father

*And Jesus, when he was baptized, went up straightway out
of the water: and, lo, the heavens were opened unto him,
and he saw the Spirit of God descending like a dove, and
lighting upon him: and lo a voice from heaven, saying,
This is my beloved Son, in whom I am well pleased.*

MATTHEW 3:16–17

Father, Jesus was baptized by John the Baptist,
as an example for us to follow.

When Jesus came out of the water, the
heavens opened. Your Spirit came down and
rested on Jesus. Your voice was heard saying,
"This is my beloved Son, in whom I am well
pleased."

You expressed Your love for Jesus and
followed that with a declaration of Your pleasure
in Him. What a beautiful picture of Your joy in
Your Son, Father.

"Father, Forgive Them"

And when they were come to the place, which is called Calvary, there they crucified him, and the malefactors, one on the right hand, and the other on the left. Then said Jesus, Father, forgive them; for they know not what they do.
LUKE 23:33–34

Lord God, it must have been agony to watch Your Son being nailed to a cross. He was hung between common criminals—two men who deserved punishment. But the innocent Jesus suffered the same penalty.

But even in the midst of an underserved death sentence, Jesus begged You to forgive the ones killing Him. Lord, Your willingness to forgive is amazing. Even with Your Son in anguish, You could forgive those who sinned against You.

Father, please help me extend forgiveness to those who hurt *me*.

One God and Father of All

*There is one body, and one Spirit, even as ye are called in
one hope of your calling; one Lord, one faith, one baptism,
one God and Father of all, who is above all,
and through all, and in you all.*
EPHESIANS 4:4–6

Lord, the apostle Paul wrote that there is "one
God and Father of all." He said that You are
"above all, and through all, and in you all."
Father, your power is so great.

I thank You that You are *above* all. You reign
supremely and hold the world in Your hands.

I thank You that You are *through* all. No
matter what touches my life, nothing can
happen outside of Your will.

I thank You that you are *in* all of Your
children. You indwell me—may I keep myself
unpolluted from the world so that Your temple
is pure.

GOODWILL

Doing Good

Do that which is good,
and thou shalt have praise of the same.
ROMANS 13:3

Lord, Your command is simple: "Do that which is good." It seems like that should be simple to carry out—but sometimes I give in to temptation. I don't do what I should. I ask Your forgiveness for the times that I fail.

Please strengthen me to do good. I want to do what is right, not just for the praise of men, but to bring You joy. You have done so many good things for me; may I do good to others for Your glory.

Overcome Evil with Good

Be not overcome of evil, but overcome evil with good.
ROMANS 12:21

Father, there is evil all around me. Satan would have loved nothing more than to keep You from sending Jesus to earth. But You will always conquer Satan—Jesus arrived that night over two thousand years ago, just as You planned. You are the victor!

Later, Satan tried to tempt Jesus—but again, You were triumphant. Ultimately, Jesus died and was resurrected for all mankind.

With that kind of power in me, I can do good to others. It is my desire to overcome evil with good.

The Gift of Time

*Pure religion and undefiled before God and the Father
is this, to visit the fatherless and widows in their affliction,
and to keep himself unspotted from the world.*
JAMES 1:27

Father, doing good to others isn't just giving
them things. I know I should give my time,
as well. All around me are the fatherless, the
widows—all of them experiencing hardships.
May I visit with them and help them in unique
ways, showing Your love as I meet their physical
needs.

Lord, I long to be "unspotted" from the
world—but sometimes I fail. Help me to remain
in You, to keep my distance from worldly things.
May I never wander away from You.

God Is Good

*Trust in the LORD, and do good; so shalt thou dwell
in the land, and verily thou shalt be fed.*
PSALM 37:3

Lord God, You are the definition of "good."
You are trustworthy—we do not doubt Your
goodness, Your love, or Your power.

In Your Word, You instructed Your people
to trust You and do good. Then they could
continue to dwell in the land, with You providing
for their daily needs.

May I trust in You and do good, as well,
Lord—but not just for Your blessing. May I
simply do that from a heart full of love for You.

Trading Good for Bad

But I say unto you, Love your enemies, bless them that curse you, do good to them that hate you, and pray for them which despitefully use you, and persecute you.
MATTHEW 5:44

Lord, it's easy to love my friends and bless those who are kind to me. I find it no chore to do good to my allies and pray for the people who treat me with respect.

But Your challenge is difficult: You ask me to love my *enemies*, to bless those who curse me, to do good to the people who hate me, to pray for those who treat me horribly.

I can't do that in my own power, Lord. So I ask that You fill me with *Your* love. May I show Your love to those who wound me.

Goodwill Toward Men

And suddenly there was with the angel a multitude of the heavenly host praising God, and saying, Glory to God in the highest, and on earth peace, good will toward men.
LUKE 2:13–14

Father, those joyful angels appeared before the shepherds, shouting their praise of You. They acknowledged that You are the highest. They declared peace for the earth and goodwill toward men.

We thank You for the goodwill You demonstrated in sending Your Son to earth. We pray that Your peace will reign on the earth. Help me to do good to others, whether they are fellow believers or not. In doing so, I show Your light to those in darkness.

THE HOLY SPIRIT

Our Comforter

*But the Comforter, which is the Holy Ghost, whom the
Father will send in my name, he shall teach you all things,
and bring all things to your remembrance,
whatsoever I have said unto you.*

JOHN 14:26

Lord, I thank You for sending us the
Comforter—Your Holy Spirit. You haven't just
sent Him to the world in general, but to me
personally.

Father, I ask that You make me teachable,
so I can learn from Your Spirit. My soul longs
for knowledge and wisdom from You. May my
mind grasp what Your Spirit wants to teach me.

Holy Spirit, I invite You to train me in the
Father's ways. Increase my understanding.

The Fruit of the Spirit

But the fruit of the Spirit is love, joy, peace,
longsuffering, gentleness, goodness, faith, meekness,
temperance: against such there is no law.
GALATIANS 5:22–23

Lord God, I want to have the fruit of Your Spirit in my life. I want it to be said of me that I am loving, joyful, peaceful, patient, gentle, good, faithful, meek, and mild.

Some days, these are difficult traits for me to master. Especially during this Christmas season, there are times I feel as if I'm not making any progress at all. But You have promised to help me. I can invite Your Spirit to fill me. I can grow in these qualities, becoming more like You each day.

Do Not Grieve the Spirit

And grieve not the holy Spirit of God,
whereby ye are sealed unto the day of redemption.
EPHESIANS 4:30

Father, I hate the thought of grieving Your Spirit. I pray that I will live in purity. May my words, thoughts, and actions be acceptable to You.

I cannot hide anything from You—You know my thoughts, You hear the words I speak, You see each and every one of my actions. When I do something that grieves Your Spirit, may I be quick to repent, so that our relationship can be restored. I want only to stay close to You and bring You joy.

My Body, God's Temple

*What? know ye not that your body is the temple of
the Holy Ghost which is in you, which ye have of God,
and ye are not your own? For ye are bought with a price:
therefore glorify God in your body, and in your spirit,
which are God's.*

1 CORINTHIANS 6:19–20

Father, we who believe in Your name have Your
Spirit living within us. Our bodies are actually
Your home. You dwell in us, having purchased
us with the shed blood of Jesus Christ.

I thank You for sending Jesus to die for
my sins. When I believed in You, You took up
residence in me. You are welcome to reign in me.

I want others to see You in me, as I allow
You to control my body and my spirit.

The Great Commission

*But ye shall receive power, after that the Holy Ghost is
come upon you: and ye shall be witnesses unto me both
in Jerusalem, and in all Judaea, and in Samaria,
and unto the uttermost part of the earth.*

ACTS 1:8

Lord, these are Your last recorded words
before You returned to heaven. You promised
Your followers that they would receive Your
power after the Holy Spirit came on them.
You told them they should take Your message
to Jerusalem, Judea, and Samaria, and to the
"uttermost part of the earth."

Father, help me to deliver Your message to
those around me—and also to those beyond my
immediate locale. I want the same excitement
and urgency the shepherds had when they
spread the good news of Jesus' birth around
Bethlehem.

You have given me new life, and I want to
share that with others.

Good Gifts, Great Gifts

If ye then, being evil, know how to give good gifts unto your children: how much more shall your heavenly Father give the Holy Spirit to them that ask him?
LUKE 11:13

Father, You eagerly await our request for the Holy Spirit. Human parents are excited about giving gifts to their children—those things they've asked for repeatedly, and others they just know the kids would enjoy. If humans can do that for their children, I can only imagine how eager You are to give such a powerful, life-changing gift.

I ask that You fill me with Your Holy Spirit today. Thank You, Lord.

HOPE

Complete Hope

If in this life only we have hope in Christ, we are of all men most miserable. But now is Christ risen from the dead, and become the firstfruits of them that slept.
1 CORINTHIANS 15:19–20

Lord God, had Jesus not died to forgive our sins, we would not have full hope. We could have only partial hope in a good man or a prophet. But because Jesus—fully man and fully God—died for us and rose from the dead, we have *complete* hope. We have been forgiven and will spend eternity with You.

All of us who follow Jesus will be resurrected with Him—and we will worship You together forever. There is no better, fuller hope.

An Expected End

For I know the thoughts that I think toward you,
saith the LORD, thoughts of peace, and not of evil,
to give you an expected end.
JEREMIAH 29:11

Lord, You have a hope for me—an "expected end." I don't know all the details of that end, but I can put my trust in You, because Your ways are perfect.

Help me not to be anxious, trying to determine what the end may be. May I rest in You as I travel the path You've laid out for me, remembering that You have specific thoughts about me and my future.

You will never lead me into evil. Nothing will come unexpectedly to You. I thank You for Your goodness.

Hoping and Quietly Waiting

The LORD is my portion, saith my soul; therefore will I hope in him. The LORD is good unto them that wait for him, to the soul that seeketh him. It is good that a man should both hope and quietly wait for the salvation of the LORD.

LAMENTATIONS 3:24–26

Father, Your Word says it's good to "both hope and quietly wait for the salvation of the Lord." I imagine that was what Mary, Jesus' mother, did—both hope and quietly wait. The angel told her that she had been chosen to give birth to Your Son, and she simply agreed to the plan. With only one question—"How is it possible for this to happen?"—she chose to both hope and quietly wait for the arrival of the Messiah.

Lord, as Your plan unfolds in my life, I will both hope and quietly wait as You work in me.

Continual Hope

But I will hope continually,
and will yet praise thee more and more.
PSALM 71:14

Lord God, the psalmist declared that he would "hope continually." There was no end to his hope, and his praise of You increased "more and more."

Father, I want to hope in You continually, as well. Forgive me for the times that I waver. You have proven that You are worthy—I'm the one who fails.

I want to increase my praise to You, both in its quantity and intensity. As I learn more of You, I will choose to praise you "more and more."

Faith and Hope

Now faith is the substance of things hoped for,
the evidence of things not seen.
HEBREWS 11:1

Father, Simeon exhibited a true faith. The Holy Spirit told Simeon that he would not die until he saw Christ. He believed the promise and waited for that great moment to arrive.

The Spirit led Simeon to the temple where he found Mary, Joseph, and Jesus. He took the baby into his arms and blessed You, acknowledging that the Spirit's promise had been fulfilled.

Lord, please give me a faith like Simeon's. He didn't know the details of the plan; he merely waited until You called on him.

May I patiently wait for Your promises, too—prepared for Your use in the work You have for me.

The Hope in God's Word

*For whatsoever things were written aforetime were
written for our learning, that we through patience
and comfort of the scriptures might have hope.*
ROMANS 15:4

Father, I thank You for giving us Your Word.
Many of Your promises have already been
fulfilled, and I wait in anticipation of what is
yet to come.

Teach me from Your Word, so I can learn
from the example of those who went before.
The scriptures were written for our learning,
with many lessons that will give me hope as I
grow closer to You. Show me what You want me
to learn today.

Thank You for the comfort of Your words,
Lord.

HOSPITALITY

Entertaining Angels

Be not forgetful to entertain strangers:
for thereby some have entertained angels unawares.
HEBREWS 13:2

Lord, there are many stories of angelic visits in Your Word: an angel delivered a message to Mary, another spoke to Joseph, and a host of angels appeared to the shepherds as they were watching their sheep at night. Each of these people knew they'd had an encounter with a messenger from You.

You tell us to be hospitable to everyone, because we might host an angel without knowing it. Help me, Lord, to treat each guest in my home as if I knew they were a heavenly being sent by You.

Willing Hospitality

Use hospitality one to another without grudging.
1 PETER 4:9

Lord God, You want me to be hospitable, but with a good attitude—not with an unwilling spirit.

Father, some of the people I invite into my home I truly enjoy. The conversation is easy and the fellowship is refreshing.

But there are others I find are more difficult to host—I eagerly await their departure. But I know that is not demonstrating hospitality "without grudging."

Please give me a willing, hospitable spirit— one that encourages every guest. May I focus on developing relationships, treating them as I would treat You.

Given to Hospitality

Be kindly affectioned one to another with brotherly love;
in honour preferring one another . . . distributing to
the necessity of saints; given to hospitality.
ROMANS 12:10, 13

Father, You've told us to love each other, honoring one another by placing their needs and wants above our own. You want us to do what we can to make certain others' needs are met through our hospitality.

At this time of year, with everything that needs to be done, hospitality can be difficult. But You've asked me to be "given" to hospitality—so with Your help, I will welcome guests into my home.

No Room at the Inn

*And she brought forth her firstborn son, and wrapped
him in swaddling clothes, and laid him in a manger;
because there was no room for them in the inn.*

LUKE 2:7

Lord God, the inn was full the night that Mary and Joseph arrived in Bethlehem. They had just finished a long journey, and Mary was ready to give birth at any time. All they wanted was a room where they could relax and rest.

Though the innkeeper couldn't provide a room for the couple, he offered the unoccupied space that he did have: the stable.

Father, I thank You for providing for our needs—even when it's in a manner different than we might expect.

Mary and Martha

*But Martha was cumbered about much serving, and came
to him, and said, Lord, dost thou not care that my sister
hath left me to serve alone? bid her therefore that she help me.
And Jesus answered and said unto her, Martha, Martha,
thou art careful and troubled about many things: but one
thing is needful: and Mary hath chosen that good part,
which shall not be taken away from her.*

LUKE 10:40–42

Father, Mary and Martha welcomed their friend
Jesus into their home. Martha worked hard for
her guest and served Him, showing attention to
His needs. But Mary simply sat with Jesus and
listened as He spoke.

When Martha approached Jesus to complain
that Mary wasn't helping with the chores, Jesus
quietly told Martha that Mary had chosen the
better of the two roles.

Father, I want to serve others—but may I
never be so busy serving that I miss spending
time with You.

A Woman from Shunem

And it fell on a day, that Elisha passed to Shunem,
where was a great woman; and she constrained him to eat
bread And so it was, that as oft as he passed by, he turned
in thither to eat bread And she said unto her husband . .
Let us make a little chamber, I pray thee, on the wall;
and let us set for him there a bed, and a table, and a stool,
and a candlestick: and it shall be, when he cometh to us,
that he shall turn in thither.
2 KINGS 4:8–10

Lord, this woman invited Your prophet to share
a meal with her family. When she realized how
often he passed by her house, she continued to
invite him in. But she didn't stop there—she
also created a private room for Elijah.

I thank You for the example of this woman
from Shunem. Please open my eyes to those
around me whom You would have me entertain,
Lord. May I see their needs and provide for
them to the best of my ability.

The Name of Jesus Prophesied

And she shall bring forth a son, and thou shalt call his name
JESUS: for he shall save his people from their sins.
MATTHEW 1:21

Lord God, an angel appeared to Joseph in a dream and detailed the plan for Jesus' arrival. The angel assured Joseph that Mary's pregnancy was legitimate: She was to give birth to the Son of God, the Messiah. And the angel instructed Joseph to name the baby *Jesus*, because He would be the one to save people from their sins.

Father, I thank You for fulfilling Your prophecy, for sending Your Son, Jesus. I thank You that He has saved us from our sins.

The Word Made Flesh

And the Word was made flesh, and dwelt among us,
(and we beheld his glory, the glory as of the only
begotten of the Father,) full of grace and truth.
JOHN 1:14

Father, Your Son took on the form of flesh—
He became human and walked this earth. He
was subject to the same physical and emotional
needs that all humans have. He was separated
from You, yet He gladly invested in the lives of
those around Him. He came not only as a Savior
but also as a friend.

I thank You, Jesus, for willingly leaving
heaven to live among men. Your sacrifice allows
us to receive the gift of forgiveness and eternal
life.

The Name of Jesus Blessed

And when eight days were accomplished for the circumcising of the child, his name was called JESUS, which was so named of the angel before he was conceived in the womb.

LUKE 2:21

Heavenly Father, You had prophesied the coming of Your Son. And an angel instructed Joseph in a dream that the baby Mary would bear should be called *Jesus.*

As a young baby, Jesus was circumcised according to Jewish tradition. Mary and Joseph then presented Him to You at the temple, officially declaring His name Jesus.

I thank You, Father, for the sweet name of Jesus. We honor the name of Your Son.

Growing in Wisdom and Stature

And Jesus increased in wisdom and stature,
and in favour with God and man.
LUKE 2:52

Lord, just like all children, Jesus grew both physically and in His knowledge of You. Your favor was on Him—as was the favor of the people around Him.

Others recognized something different about this man, though many could not define that special quality. This was a boy who was developing physically into a man, but who was also profound in His knowledge of You and Your scriptures.

May I continue to grow in my knowledge of You, as well—so that You and others will look on me with favor.

The Author and Finisher of Our Faith

Let us run with patience the race that is set before us,
looking unto Jesus the author and finisher of our faith;
who for the joy that was set before him endured the cross,
despising the shame, and is set down at the
right hand of the throne of God.
HEBREWS 12:1–2

Father God, You sent Jesus to earth as a baby. Your perfect plan required Him to die on the cross then rise again for the sins of mankind.

I thank You for giving us Jesus, the "author and finisher of our faith." He became the sacrifice for us, to make us guiltless in Your eyes. His death and Resurrection completed the work You had for Him.

Jesus, You endured the cross and its shame for me. May I never take Your sacrifice for granted.

The Return to Heaven

Which also said, Ye men of Galilee,
why stand ye gazing up into heaven? this same Jesus,
which is taken up from you into heaven, shall so come
in like manner as ye have seen him go into heaven.
ACTS 1:11

Father, when Jesus returned to heaven, You sent an angel to minister to those who witnessed His departure. In a time of confusion, the angel spoke peace to them. The angel declared where Jesus had gone, and said He would one day return in the same manner.

This was a moment of hope, Father: Jesus had returned to heaven to be with You, but He would come back again someday.

I thank You for that message of hope. We eagerly await Your return.

JOY

Fullness of Joy

*Thou wilt shew me the path of life: in thy presence
is fulness of joy; at thy right hand there are
pleasures for evermore.*
PSALM 16:11

Lord God, during this season of joy, I want to dwell in Your presence and experience full joy. I am thankful for the celebration of Jesus' Nativity. May I continue to celebrate through the entire year, not stopping when Christmas has past.

I thank You that You have a "path of life" for me, and that I have already experienced the joy of becoming Your child. I anticipate future joy as I draw even closer to You.

Father, I thank You for the endless joy that we will celebrate in heaven.

Tidings of Great Joy

And the angel said unto them, Fear not: for, behold,
I bring you good tidings of great joy,
which shall be to all people.

LUKE 2:10

Father, the angel told the shepherds not to be afraid, because he was bringing a *joyful* message. The message was one for the benefit of all people: A Savior had been born.

Then many angels joined together for a celebration in the skies above Bethlehem. Their praises to You inspired the shepherds to go immediately to Bethlehem to find the baby.

Lord God, I thank You for the joy surrounding Jesus' birth. I desire to seek You with the same joy and purpose the shepherds had that night.

Rejoice. . .and Rejoice Again

Rejoice in the Lord always: and again I say, Rejoice.
PHILIPPIANS 4:4

Lord God, You desire that we Christians live with a spirit of joy. We can be joyful even when friends disappoint us, a loved one dies, we lose employment, or we experience health issues. You walk through each hardship with us—and in that, we can be joyful.

When those difficulties come, may I focus on Your love and care for me. Then, even in painful circumstances, I can rest in You and know the joy of the Lord.

A Joyful Wedding Celebration

I will greatly rejoice in the LORD, my soul shall be joyful in my God; for he hath clothed me with the garments of salvation, he hath covered me with the robe of righteousness, as a bridegroom decketh himself with ornaments, and as a bride adorneth herself with her jewels.

ISAIAH 61:10

Heavenly Father, a wedding is a joyful thing. The bride and groom have eagerly awaited the day that they will be husband and wife. Both dress in special clothing made specifically for the occasion. There are music, food, friends, and family to enjoy. The uniting of a man and woman in Christ is cause for celebration.

You, Lord, have called the church Your bride. We anticipate that joyful day when we are united with You, to be with You throughout eternity.

Less Sorrow, More Joy

And the ransomed of the LORD shall return,
and come to Zion with songs and everlasting joy upon
their heads: they shall obtain joy and gladness,
and sorrow and sighing shall flee away.
ISAIAH 35:10

Lord God, please make my soul joyful in You. You have sent Your Son to save me from my sins, and now You call me Your child. Because of what You have done for me, I will sing songs of praise to You.

Please keep my heart full of gladness. Replace my sorrow with joy. You have declared that I belong to You, so I have no reason to fear. No one can take me away from You.

I rejoice in You! May I live my life so that You can rejoice in me.

Filled with Joy

When they saw the star,
they rejoiced with exceeding great joy.
MATTHEW 2:10

Father, the wise men had taken a long journey, following a star they had seen from a distance. Their quest took them to Jerusalem, where they asked King Herod for the location of the King of the Jews. When they left the king, they again saw the star and followed it, being filled with joy.

Lord, I thank You for Your direction. May I follow Your path with a joyful spirit, trusting that You will lead me always in Your way.

LOVE

A Loving Heart

And now, Israel, what doth the LORD thy God require of thee, but to fear the LORD thy God, to walk in all his ways, and to love him, and to serve the LORD thy God with all thy heart and with all thy soul.

DEUTERONOMY 10:12

Heavenly Father, Your Word says You "require" my love—but I don't love You from obligation. I love you with a grateful heart!

To demonstrate my love, I will respect You, walk in Your ways, and serve You with my whole heart and soul. Though You are worthy of so much more love than I am capable of giving, You are satisfied with all I have to give.

I love You, Lord. Thank You for loving me first.

Complete Love

*Jesus said unto him, Thou shalt love the Lord thy God with
all thy heart, and with all thy soul, and with all thy mind.
This is the first and great commandment. And the second is
like unto it, Thou shalt love thy neighbour as thyself.*
MATTHEW 22:37–39

Lord God, Jesus commanded that we love You
with all our heart, soul, and mind. He said that
was the greatest commandment.

But He mentioned a second commandment,
which is often more challenging. I am to love my
neighbor with the same love I have for myself.
Sometimes, I can obey that command. But what
about those people who are unkind to me?

Please fill me with Your love so that it
overflows to those around me—even the ones
who are difficult to love.

A Definition of Love

Charity suffereth long, and is kind; charity envieth not; charity vaunteth not itself, is not puffed up, doth not behave itself unseemly, seeketh not her own, is not easily provoked, thinketh no evil; rejoiceth not in iniquity, but rejoiceth in the truth; beareth all things, believeth all things, hopeth all things, endureth all things. Charity never faileth.

1 CORINTHIANS 13:4–8

Lord, You've clearly shown us what love is and what it is not.

If I show love, I will be patient and kind. I won't envy, boast, or demonstrate pride. I will behave properly and won't try to get my own way. I will keep hold of my temper and give no place to evil. I will not be joyful in any sinful situation, but I will rejoice in the truth. I will protect, trust, hope, and persevere.

Lord, please make me a truly loving person to those around me today.

Reminder to Love

Let all your things be done with charity.
1 CORINTHIANS 16:14

Father God, if everything were done from a heart of love, the wickedness in the world would disappear. We would not seek our own way from a heart of pride. We would not harbor anger toward others. We would cheer others on, even if that meant we were to lose.

Please help me to have love for others. When I am tempted to push for my own way, remind me to love. When I become angry, remind me to love. And even if it looks as if I'll lose, remind me to love. I want to follow Your example, showing love to others unconditionally.

A Mother's Love

Beloved, let us love one another: for love is of God;
and every one that loveth is born of God, and knoweth God.
1 JOHN 4:7

Father, I thank You for sending Your gift of love to the world so long ago. You sent Your love in the form of Your Son, Jesus.

Mary must have overflowed with love, realizing that she was not only holding her baby, but the Savior of the world. Her heart must have been full as she comprehended her own role in sharing Your gift of love with the world.

Love has its origin in You, Lord. I offer all of my love to You; please help me to extend that love to others.

Love in Words and Deeds

My little children, let us not love in word,
neither in tongue; but in deed and in truth.
1 JOHN 3:18

Lord God, it's easy to say those three little words thoughtlessly: "I love you." But You want us to show a depth of our love in our *actions*. You want our deeds to demonstrate the love that is within us.

Father, help me to speak my love intentionally, but also to show it by my deeds. May others know that I am Your child simply by observing the love I share.

With a sincere heart, I proclaim, "I love You!"

MONEY

Two Masters

No man can serve two masters: for either he will hate the one, and love the other; or else he will hold to the one, and despise the other. Ye cannot serve God and mammon.
MATTHEW 6:24

Lord, money can certainly distract us. It can turn our eyes away from You, toward fulfilling our own desires. Your Word says that we will either choose to serve You or we will choose to serve money—we can't divide our attention equally.

I thank You for Your provision, Father. Help me to view money as a gift from You to meet my needs and to share with others. Protect me from the temptation to "serve" money. I will only be truly successful when my priorities are in the right place.

The Love of Money

For the love of money is the root of all evil: which while some coveted after, they have erred from the faith, and pierced themselves through with many sorrows.
1 TIMOTHY 6:10

Father God, many have misquoted Your Word, saying that "*money* is the root of all evil." But it doesn't say that. It says that the "*love* of money" is the problem.

I don't want money to be more important than my relationships with others. . .or with You. You have given me all that I have—help me to hold it with an open hand.

I ask that You give me the proper perspective on how to spend and share my money. I want to be generous and bless others with what You have given me.

Conversation Check

*Let your conversation be without covetousness; and be
content with such things as ye have: for he hath said,
I will never leave thee, nor forsake thee.*
HEBREWS 13:5

Lord, in the old language of the King James
Version, "conversation" means "way of life." But
it's interesting that our speech, too, can be filled
with covetousness.

Father, may my speech be free of envy and
greed. I pray that I'll keep a healthy perspective
on money. I want to be content with what You
have given me, rather than preoccupied with
how I can get more.

Thank You for the promise that You will
never leave me nor forsake me. Help me to train
my mind on that security.

Prayers and Promises *for* Christmas 107

Treasures of Heaven

Lay not up for yourselves treasures upon earth, where moth
and rust doth corrupt, and where thieves break through and
steal: but lay up for yourselves treasures in heaven, where
neither moth nor rust doth corrupt, and where thieves
do not break through nor steal: for where your treasure is,
there will your heart be also.
MATTHEW 6:19–21

Father, many treasures tempt me here on earth. I am bombarded with advertisements for the newest and best of everything. But the things of this earth are temporary. They break, they're lost, they're stolen. So why should I spend my time trying to accumulate more?

I choose the treasures of *heaven*—those things that cannot break, become lost, or get stolen. I want to fix my heart on the things of heaven, rather than those on earth.

Seeking His Kingdom

*Therefore take no thought, saying, What shall we eat? or,
What shall we drink? or, Wherewithal shall we be clothed?
(For after all these things do the Gentiles seek:) for your
heavenly Father knoweth that ye have need of all these things.
But seek ye first the kingdom of God, and his righteousness;
and all these things shall be added unto you.*
MATTHEW 6:31–33

Lord, there is so much to consider during this Christmas season. We want to eat special foods and enjoy festive events. There are decorations to put up and gifts to buy.

But You warn us against worrying over such things—You say to "take no thought" of them. When matters of money and possessions consume our thoughts, we are not keeping our priorities in order.

Before I make purchases this Christmas, Lord, may I take time to seek Your kingdom, those things that are of eternal value. May Your righteousness reign in me.

Monetary Blessings

He that trusteth in his riches shall fall;
but the righteous shall flourish as a branch.
PROVERBS 11:28

Lord, You have promised blessing to those who do not trust in their wealth. And You have cautioned that those who do put their trust in riches will fall.

I thank You for Your blessings, Father. I want to put my full trust in You, not in anything of this world. Wealth is only temporary, so I will choose to invest in things that matter eternally. Please guide me to those people with whom I can share the riches of Your Word—the only kind of riches that will last forever.

MUSIC

A New Song of Praise

O sing unto the LORD a new song; for he hath done marvellous things: his right hand, and his holy arm, hath gotten him the victory.
PSALM 98:1

Father, You have done many marvelous things for me. . .too many to count. You have saved me, You protect me, and You love me. You bless me with good friends and the provision I need for each day. You call me Your friend. Your ways are too wonderful for me to comprehend.

You are victorious. You have overcome death and have conquered evil. I sing a new song of praise to You today, for You deserve my praise.

Singing Merrily

Is any among you afflicted? let him pray.
Is any merry? let him sing psalms.
JAMES 5:13

Lord God, we use the word "merry" so much at Christmastime, it's become commonplace. We say "Merry Christmas" to everyone we meet. We hear "We Wish You a Merry Christmas" seemingly everywhere we go.

We should be merry at this time of year— but may we always be merry in You, because of all You have done for us. I lift my song of praise to You, because You fill me with joy.

Earthly Music, Heavenly Music

*Be filled with the Spirit; speaking to yourselves in psalms
and hymns and spiritual songs, singing and
making melody in your heart to the Lord.*
EPHESIANS 5:18–19

Lord, please fill me with Your Spirit. What will flow out from me is praise to You, songs from my heart that I will sing to my Lord.

Father, I thank You for music. It's a beautiful background for whatever I do. But the music of earth is just practice for what we will experience in heaven with You. Countless voices will join with the angels' in praise to You.

I long to add my voice to that choir, worshipping You throughout eternity.

The Gift of Music

*Let the word of Christ dwell in you richly in all wisdom;
teaching and admonishing one another in psalms and
hymns and spiritual songs, singing with grace
in your hearts to the Lord.*
COLOSSIANS 3:16

Father, Your Word should dwell in us so that we can grow in wisdom. We can read scriptures and hear others teach on them—but we can also use songs to grow in our spiritual walk.

What a joy to hear youngsters sing the songs they've learned in Sunday school. "Jesus Loves Me, This I Know. . . ." And when I'm going through a difficult time, how encouraging it is to have a hymn or chorus come to mind.

I thank You for the teaching that comes through song—and I offer up my gift of musical praise to You.

A Song of Worship

*O come, let us sing unto the LORD: let us make
a joyful noise to the rock of our salvation.*
PSALM 95:1

Lord, during the season of celebrating Your birth, many songs are lifted in praise to You. Some are older, more traditional tunes; others more recent. There are occasions to go caroling, sing in a church service, or attend a concert. Help me, Lord, not to be concerned with "performance," but instead to focus on worshipping You.

You don't care whether our pitch is angelic. You simply delight in our praise—the offering of our hearts to You. May you be blessed by my musical gift of praise.

A Song of Praise

I will sing unto the LORD as long as I live:
I will sing praise to my God while I have my being.
PSALM 104:33

Father, You desire my praise. With the psalmist, I declare that I will sing to You for as long as You give me breath. For all the days I have on this earth, I will sing to You.

My sacrifice of praise will be on my lips continually. I will sing of Your love, Your salvation, and Your promises. You have given me many blessings, and I will bless Your name in song.

May You be glorified through my song of praise.

THE POOR

A Soft Heart and Open Hand

If there be among you a poor man of one of thy brethren within any of thy gates in thy land which the LORD thy God giveth thee, thou shalt not harden thine heart, nor shut thine hand from thy poor brother: But thou shalt open thine hand wide unto him, and shalt surely lend him sufficient for his need, in that which he wanteth.

DEUTERONOMY 15:7–8

Lord God, there are people who are poor because of the choices they've made, and there are others who find themselves poor from uncontrollable circumstances. But You don't make those distinctions. Forgive me for the times I've tried to determine the cause of a person's poverty, judging rather than helping.

Soften my heart, Lord, and teach me to approach the poor with an open hand. May I be willing and prepared to give from the blessings You have given me.

No Rush to Judgment

Ye shall do no unrighteousness in judgment:
thou shalt not respect the person of the poor,
nor honor the person of the mighty:
but in righteousness shalt thou judge thy neighbour.
LEVITICUS 19:15

Lord, I have been guilty of showing favoritism. I don't always mean to, but my mind can formulate thoughts about others that just aren't true.

Father, I don't want to treat people disrespectfully because they are considered "poor." Nor do I want to honor people because they are well off. Money makes no difference in Your eyes—Your judgment is rooted in righteousness.

Teach me to consider others from Your righteous point of view rather than one based on social status. Forgive me for the times I fail.

Lending to the Lord

He that hath pity upon the poor lendeth unto the LORD;
and that which he hath given will he pay him again.
PROVERBS 19:17

Father God, this Christmas I ask that You open my eyes to a person in need. Give me compassion for someone who is poor. I want to be Your hands and feet, to fill a need for someone.

Thank You for the blessing You have proclaimed to those who help the poor. I don't want to give so I can get a blessing in return—but I thank You for those times You do bless me.

May I be sensitive to those in need around me and see them through Your eyes.

A Widow's Mite

He saw also a certain poor widow casting in thither two
mites. And he said, Of a truth I say unto you, that this poor
widow hath cast in more than they all: For all these have
of their abundance cast in unto the offerings of God: but
she of her penury hath cast in all the living that she had.
LUKE 21:2–4

Father, Jesus spoke of a very poor woman—yet
she gave what she had. She didn't rationalize,
thinking she didn't need to give because she
didn't have much.

May I learn from her example, Lord. I want
to give what I have to You.

You expect me to be wise with my money,
to meet my financial obligations. But please
teach me to give not only "out of abundance." I
should give of all that I have.

A Request for Compassion

For thou hast been a strength to the poor,
a strength to the needy in his distress,
a refuge from the storm, a shadow from the heat,
when the blast of the terrible ones is
as a storm against the wall.
ISAIAH 25:4

Father, during this Christmas season, please make me aware of those who lack a home—who need a "refuge from the storm."

Many people are working hard to change their circumstances. . .but need someone else to be their "strength." Please give me Your power so that I can make a difference in the lives of others. I want to help those who are distressed—and in doing so, demonstrate how much I love You.

Consider the Poor

Blessed is he that considereth the poor: the LORD will deliver him in time of trouble. The LORD will preserve him, and keep him alive; and he shall be blessed upon the earth: and thou wilt not deliver him unto the will of his enemies.

PSALM 41:1–2

Lord God, there are poor people all around me. Sometimes it's obvious by their dress; other times I see it in their eyes. Others hide it better.

Please use me, Father, to bring comfort to the poor. Give me insight so I know the best way to assist them. Open my eyes to their needs.

I thank You for Your blessing on those who help the poor. Bless those whom I'm helping, as well.

PROMISES

Great and Precious Promises

Whereby are given unto us exceeding great and precious promises: that by these ye might be partakers of the divine nature, having escaped the corruption that is in the world through lust.

2 PETER 1:4

Father, the Bible is full of promises that You have given Your children through history. You have promised rewards for obedience and consequences for disobedience. You have promised to protect and care for Your children.

I rest in Your promises today, Lord. I know that I can trust You to accomplish each one—because You are a God of truth. I thank You for each one of Your precious promises.

Pure Promises

Having therefore these promises, dearly beloved,
let us cleanse ourselves from all filthiness of the flesh
and spirit, perfecting holiness in the fear of God
2 Corinthians 7:1

Lord, Your promises are pure. And before I open Your Word, I ask that You cleanse my heart of any wickedness—anything that is contrary to Your Spirit. I want to be pure in spirit and approach Your holy scriptures with fear, a deep reverence for the words that You have given to us.

May my eyes be open to what You are saying to me through Your Word. May it renew my heart.

Promises Fulfilled

God is not a man, that he should lie; neither the son of man,
that he should repent: hath he said, and shall he not do it?
or hath he spoken, and shall he not make it good?
NUMBERS 23:19

Lord Jesus, You came to earth as a human being, but You were not only man—You were God *and* man. As God, You cannot lie. You never had to repent, because You did not sin. I know I can believe that You will do whatever You say, since You are capable only of truth and goodness.

I thank You for sharing Your promises with us. We are then able to see Your hand at work, as You fulfill each promise You have given. You are truly good!

True Words

The Lord is not slack concerning his promise,
as some men count slackness; but is longsuffering
to us-ward, not willing that any should perish,
but that all should come to repentance.

2 PETER 3:9

Father, if You say You're going to do something, it will be done. You haven't made any promise that You don't intend to keep.

Lord, I ask that I will consider what I promise in the same way. May I think before I make a promise. May I follow through with everything I say I'll do. May my words be true, so that I can be a pure reflection of You.

Promises to Heroes

These all died in faith, not having received the promises, but having seen them afar off, and were persuaded of them, and embraced them, and confessed that they were strangers and pilgrims on the earth.
HEBREWS 11:13

Lord God, in the book of Hebrews, You've honored many heroes of the faith. Some had seen a few of Your promises fulfilled, but they died with other promises outstanding. But they believed that You would keep Your promises.

Please increase my faith so that I can believe You, even if I do not see an immediate answer. You will certainly keep all Your promises—so help me not to doubt. Your Word is truth.

A New Home

In my Father's house are many mansions: if it were not so,
I would have told you. I go to prepare a place for you.
And if I go and prepare a place for you, I will come again,
and receive you unto myself; that where I am,
there ye may be also.
JOHN 14:2–3

Father, during the Christmas season, I enjoy the decorations in my and others' homes. There are festive trees, bright lights, Nativity scenes, and lawn decorations everywhere we turn.

But You have promised a much more special place for those who give their lives to You. You are even now preparing that place for Your followers—a place of eternal light, golden streets, and boundless gems. I eagerly anticipate seeing *Your* decorated home, the one You have prepared for us. I plan to enjoy it with You forever!

SAVIOR

Birth Announcement

And the angel said unto them, Fear not: for, behold,
I bring you good tidings of great joy, which shall be to all
people. For unto you is born this day in the city of
David a Saviour, which is Christ the Lord.
LUKE 2:10–11

Lord, the shepherds received a spectacular message that night. An angel appeared, telling them not to be afraid, because he had joyful news for them. They were given a few details— who had been born, when He had arrived, and where they could find Him.

Father, may I be like the shepherds—who immediately got up to meet the Savior. Then they couldn't keep quiet, telling everyone they could about what they had seen. Give me the passion to seek You then share what I learn with those around me.

The Savior Foretold

*And it shall be for a sign and for a witness unto the LORD of
hosts in the land of Egypt: for they shall cry unto the LORD
because of the oppressors, and he shall send them a saviour,
and a great one, and he shall deliver them.*

ISAIAH 19:20

Father God, You foretold the coming of the
Savior through Your prophets. The arrival of
this Deliverer was highly anticipated. Those
who trusted in You were prepared for a glorious
advent.

The glorious advent certainly occurred—
though it was quite different than most were
expecting. There was no pomp and circumstance;
on a quiet night, far from home, in a stable, a
baby was born. But it was no ordinary birth—
the Savior of the world had come!

I thank You, Lord, that You always fulfill
Your prophecies. We can trust that You will
always keep Your Word.

The One True Savior

I, even I, am the LORD;
and beside me there is no saviour.
ISAIAH 43:11

Lord, this is such a brief, yet powerful, statement. You are the Lord—and there is no Savior other than You. You are above all creation, and there will never be any other God.

Thank You for coming to save us. We acknowledge that you are the true Savior. Thank You for Your gift of salvation and that You are preparing a special place where Your followers can live with You eternally. We look forward to seeing You and worshipping You. You alone are worthy of the love and praise due the one true Savior.

Mary's Song

And Mary said, My soul doth magnify the Lord,
and my spirit hath rejoiced in God my Saviour.
LUKE 1:46–47

Lord God, we read that Jesus' mother declared her Son "Saviour" before He was even born. After Mary learned of the miracle that was to take place, she praised You for choosing *her* to have a role in the birth of the Savior of the world.

Mary knew the Savior was coming. She knew that things would no longer be the same. But rather than fear or question, she chose to praise You for Your goodness—both to her and to all humanity. Mary rejoiced in God her Savior—and we rejoice in You, our God and Savior, too.

Savior of the World

Now we believe, not because of thy saying: for we have heard him ourselves, and know that this is indeed the Christ, the Saviour of the world.

JOHN 4:42

Father, You are truly the Savior of the world. You did not come for a particular race or gender, or a certain segment of society. You came for *all* people. After the Samaritan woman at the well spoke with Jesus, other Samaritans came to Him and believed—though Samaritans and Jews were traditionally enemies. In speaking with one woman, You brought unity to two groups.

Thank You, Lord, for saving us from our sins, for unifying us with each other and drawing us close to You. Only the Savior of the world has that power.

Savior Sacrifice

*The God of our fathers raised up Jesus, whom ye slew
and hanged on a tree. Him hath God exalted with his
right hand to be a Prince and a Saviour, for to give
repentance to Israel, and forgiveness of sins.*

ACTS 5:30–31

Father God, Your plan to physically separate
Yourself from Jesus must have been so difficult.
In many ways, the birth of Jesus was cause for
celebration and joy—but just a few years later,
the joy became persecution, then execution.
And You had to turn Your back on Jesus because
of our sins.

Father, please forgive me for my sins. I confess
that because of what I've done, I am responsible
for Your Son's death. But I thank You for being
willing to take my guilt on Yourself so I can be
saved from those sins. You are my loving Savior,
the one I love!

A Heart of Service

And ye shall serve the LORD your God,
and he shall bless thy bread, and thy water;
and I will take sickness away from the midst of thee.
EXODUS 23:25

Lord, You have blessed us in so many ways and You continue to do so. I thank You for those blessings. You have given us so much more than we deserve, and I do not take that for granted.

I want to bless You with my heart of service—not so that You will bless me, but so You will receive honor. During this season of gift-giving, I will give you my gift of service. I choose to serve You. Direct me in the way that I can best do that, Lord.

Serving in Sincerity and Truth

Now therefore fear the LORD, and serve him in sincerity
and in truth: and put away the gods which your fathers
served on the other side of the flood, and in Egypt;
and serve ye the LORD.
JOSHUA 24:14

Father, it's so easy to condemn those who
follow false gods. Sometimes I've claimed—
arrogantly—that I would never do that. Yet
there are many types of "gods" that can draw me
in, causing my desire to serve You to wane. But
You are to be the only one worth pursuing.

Throughout these hurried weeks, Father,
keep my eyes focused on You. May my mind not
wander to other things that will detract from
You. I choose to serve You "in sincerity and in
truth."

Humble Service

Whosoever will be chief among you, let him be your servant:
even as the Son of man came not to be ministered unto,
but to minister, and to give his life a ransom for many.
MATTHEW 20:27–28

Lord, You came to be a servant—that is clear even in Your humble birth. You weren't born in a palace. . .You were laid in a feeding trough for animals. There wasn't any royal birth announcement. . .the news was spread by humble men who were tending sheep that night.

It's amazing how Your plan for humanity's salvation began. In humility, You came to serve the ones who would eventually put You to death. You ministered to us so that we can live forever. We praise, honor, and exalt You!

An Example of Service

But ye shall not be so: but he that is greatest among you,
let him be as the younger; and he that is chief,
as he that doth serve.

LUKE 22:26

Father, the world's way is that the greater rules over the lesser. . .the older rules over the younger. . . the boss rules over the worker.

But Your Word teaches that true service is exactly the opposite: The greater should serve the lesser, the older should serve the younger, and the boss should serve the worker. The world laughs at the idea—but You always have the best ideas, Lord.

I thank You for leading us by example—for showing us how to serve. May I exemplify the service that Your followers should demonstrate.

Serving with Freedom

For, brethren, ye have been called unto liberty;
only use not liberty for an occasion to the flesh,
but by love serve one another.
GALATIANS 5:13

Lord, I thank You for giving me freedom.

May I never misuse that freedom by claiming I can now do whatever I want. Freedom in You is the ability to choose what is holy, what will bring You honor. Others claim that's not true freedom—but they don't understand the liberty I have from sin. You desire what is best for me, and You've provided it.

With the freedom You give me, I will choose to serve others, to raise You up. I will not serve to bring honor to myself—rather that You will be praised.

The Reward for Service

And there shall be no more curse: but the throne of God and of the Lamb shall be in it; and his servants shall serve him: and they shall see his face; and his name shall be in their foreheads.

REVELATION 22:3–4

Father God, You have promised that those who serve You will one day see Your face. Those who saw Jesus' face as a baby were instantly changed. The shepherds rejoiced. The wise men worshipped. One look at Your face altered lives forever.

We look forward with great anticipation to that moment we see Your face. It will far exceed our imagination. At the end of our service to You on earth, we will be joined in gathering around Your throne, seeing You face-to-face.

I thank You in advance for that gift!

TRADITIONS

The Meaning of Christmas

*And these words, which I command thee this day, shall be
in thine heart: and thou shalt teach them diligently unto
thy children, and shalt talk of them when thou sittest in
thine house, and when thou walkest by the way, and when
thou liest down, and when thou risest up. And thou shalt
bind them for a sign upon thine hand, and they shall be as
frontlets between thine eyes. And thou shalt write them
upon the posts of thy house, and on thy gates.*
DEUTERONOMY 6:6–9

Lord God, in the busyness of my Christmas
preparations, I sometime fail to do what You've
commanded. There are so many errands to
run, so many chores to be accomplished—and
meditation on You gets pushed back to "later,"
when my schedule permits.

Please remind me this season to be inten-
tional about You, always recalling what You
have done for me. May my thoughts constantly
turn to Your love and Your blessings, Father. I
do not want busyness to divert my attention
from the true meaning of this season.

Godly Traditions

*Beware lest any man spoil you through philosophy
and vain deceit, after the tradition of men, after the
rudiments of the world, and not after Christ.*
COLOSSIANS 2:8

Father, may I never be drawn away to follow traditions of men rather than following Christ. I've told myself that could never happen. Yet the world can easily pull me its direction, away from You.

In humility, Lord, I repent of those times I've followed the traditions of men. Some are harmless enough by themselves, but they can take my eyes from You if I'm not careful. May my focus always be on You. May all I do bring You glory and honor.

Standing Fast

Therefore, brethren, stand fast, and hold the traditions which ye have been taught, whether by word, or our epistle.
2 THESSALONIANS 2:15

Lord, I thank You for Your Word. It teaches us about You. It has been passed down from generation to generation, and we are blessed to hear Your truth.

Help me to "stand fast" in Your traditions. I can't do that on my own—I need to be firmly rooted in You.

Those traditions I've learned from You, Lord, I will pass on to others. I will not keep Your good news silent. Just as the shepherds shared their message with joy, I will continue to tell others of what You have done for me.

Obedient Traditions

Be ye followers of me, even as I also am of Christ.
Now I praise you, brethren, that ye remember me in all
things, and keep the ordinances, as I delivered them to you.
1 CORINTHIANS 11:1–2

Father, I have chosen to follow You, to obey Your commands. You have asked me to observe "the ordinances" of this faith.

You desire that Your followers be baptized, showing that their sin has been put to death and they have been raised to new life.

You have given instructions for Communion, to help me remember Jesus' death and Resurrection until He comes again.

Give me the grace to do all that You have asked me to do.

Spreading Traditions

And the things that thou hast heard of me among many witnesses, the same commit thou to faithful men, who shall be able to teach others also.
2 TIMOTHY 2:2

Lord, You've allowed me to learn about You through Your Word and the teaching of godly people. I thank You for that privilege.

Help me to encourage my family and friends to study Your Word, to sit under holy teachers. Then Your message can be delivered from one generation to the next.

When You call on me to teach others, Father, fill me with Your Spirit so that I might make Your message clear. I ask for strength to fulfill that responsibility.

From Generation to Generation

And that from a child thou hast known the holy scriptures,
which are able to make thee wise unto salvation
through faith which is in Christ Jesus.
2 TIMOTHY 3:15

Lord God, from the time we are children, we can read Your scriptures and learn to walk in Your ways. Your Word teaches us of Your character and Your love. We learn of how You came to earth as a baby in a manger, grew to manhood, and died on the cross for our sins. The Bible teaches us that we can be reconciled to You and enjoy the reward of heaven with You forever.

I thank You for Your Word. May I teach others what I have learned in its pages.

WORSHIP

Joyful Noise

Make a joyful noise unto the LORD, all ye lands.
Serve the LORD with gladness: come before
his presence with singing.
PSALM 100:1–2

Father, there are many ways we can worship You. One obvious way is music. We sing songs and play instruments to praise You. You welcome the joyful noise that we give as an offering of worship.

But, as the psalm writer says, we can also *serve* You with gladness. We can show our adoration, and bring You glory, by serving. May I serve in a spirit of gladness so that my worship is acceptable to You.

Communal Worship

O come, let us worship and bow down:
let us kneel before the LORD our maker.
PSALM 95:6

Lord God, I know You are blessed when I join other Christians in worshipping You. During this time of year, I can attend many programs and services. But I don't want to be someone who simply *attends* a worship service—I want to join in lifting up praise to You.

You seem to enjoy the worship of groups—the angels praised You together when they announced Jesus' birth to the shepherds. . .the shepherds bowed to You when they arrived at the stable. . .the wise men offered gifts when they completed their journey.

May our communal worship bring You the praise You deserve.

My Personal Worship

Give unto the LORD the glory due unto his name:
bring an offering, and come before him: worship
the LORD in the beauty of holiness.
1 CHRONICLES 16:29

Father, Your name is due an abundance of glory—more than I could ever offer. But I will bring the offering of worship that only I can give.

On that night outside Bethlehem, the angels led the shepherds in worshipping You. But it didn't stop there—the shepherds hurried to carry their worship into Your presence. And then they took to the streets to share their joy throughout the town.

May I come into Your presence with such joy, Father, and then share it freely with those around me.

A Gift of Worship

Where is he that is born King of the Jews?
for we have seen his star in the east, and are come to
worship him. . . . And when they were come into the house,
they saw the young child with Mary his mother,
and fell down, and worshipped him.
MATTHEW 2:2, 11

Lord, the wise men traveled a long distance, undoubtedly experiencing obstacles on their way—but they continued, making the journey to worship You. I want to be like those men, Father, determined to give You the worship You deserve.

I thank You that I'm not expected to worship You in a certain way, at a certain place or time. Your only desire is that I come to You humbly, worshipping You for who You are. I do that today, Father.

A Living Sacrifice

*I beseech you therefore, brethren, by the mercies of God,
that ye present your bodies a living sacrifice, holy,
acceptable unto God, which is your reasonable service.*
ROMANS 12:1

Father God, I want to obey Your Word by presenting my body to You as a living sacrifice.

In the Old Testament, Your people presented sacrifices to You. But with Your gift of Jesus Christ came a new way of sacrifice—now You ask for me!

I know You want me to willingly offer myself to You, Father, setting myself apart for Your work in me. Jesus gave His life for me; I want You to use the life You've blessed me with for Your purposes.

Lord, I freely offer the gift of myself to You.

Eternal Worship

And all the angels stood round about the throne,
and about the elders and the four beasts,
and fell before the throne on their faces,
and worshipped God.
REVELATION 7:11

Father, all of us who have been forgiven will one day worship You in heaven. We will join with the angels and all the other believers in bowing on our knees around Your throne.

But I don't want my worship to wait for that time. I bow my heart to You now and praise You for Your love, for Your gift of salvation. I thank You for sending Your Son to earth to be the sacrifice for my sins.

I am overwhelmed with my love for You, Lord. I will worship You now and throughout eternity.

Scripture Index

Also in the

PRAYERS AND PROMISES

product line:

Prayers & Promises for Women

ISBN 978-1-61626-695-0

4.375" x 6" • 224 pages • Flexible binding • $9.99

Experience a deeper and more meaningful connection to your heavenly Father with this brand-new gift edition of *Prayers & Promises for Women*. Featuring 200 devotional "prayer starters," organized into 50 practical topics—including beauty, children, forgiveness, patience, self-worth, trust, and wisdom—*Prayers & Promises for Women* provides just the hope and encouragement you need for any area of life.